PREFACE

Rock music at its origin, played with a few instruments (usually guitars, bass, drums and the singer's voice), has two fundamental characteristics, that of transformation and Mixing. *The transformation in rhythm, in the type of sound, in the timbre and effects of the instruments used, which as we will see in the first chapters,* from blues we moved on to rock and roll *and then to real rock music is its own. The mixing, that is, the ability to merge, blend with other musical genres very easily, giving rise to other genres and subgenres. The new styles that have been formed during its evolution from birth to the present day, are many and the most varied, often generating confusion for the listener, but also for those who play this type of music. It started with the Blues, until it reached alternative metal, going through hard rock and heavy metal. But also pop rock, electronic rock, root rock, industrial rock, gothic rock, etc... I've done just a few examples of the most famous genres, but also of the strangest ones. You will find them all reading the book from start to finish. That's why I wanted to write it, to describe them and put them in order of appearance, to understand how they were born, so as to create clarity to fans of this type of music.*

The description is also very technical with a careful analysis from an instrumental point of view, this was possible because I am a musician who above all listened, watched on TV and also live the concerts of the protagonists. Then also played and composed of songs. The book is a fantastic adventure also because in addition to the description of the styles, all the protagonists are cited gradually, also discovering their origin, their most beautiful songs, all accompanied by suggestive images. For each musical style or chosen two or three bands or singers who fully represented it, and which I listened to the most, precisely to take care of its technical aspect. If someone is missing, the reason is this, and also for not being too verbose.

TOPICS OF THE BOOK

- PRESENTATION
- HISTORY AND BIRTH OF THE ROCK
- THE FIRST PROTAGONISTS
- PROTAGONISTS (Rock Blues and Rock and Roll)
- EVOLUTIONS OF THE ROCK
- OTHER HARD ROCK BANDS
- PSYCHEDELIC ROCK AND PROGRESSIVE ROCK
- GRUNGE AND PUNK ROCK
- HEAVY METAL AND THRASH METAL
- POP ROCK AND NEW WAVE
- BANDS WITH OTHER ROCK FEATURES
- ALTERNATIVE ROCK
- DARK ROCK AND GOTHIC ROCK
- THE ELECTRONIC ROCK
- BEE GEES, BETWEEN POP, DISCO MUSIC AND ROCK
- GLAM ROCK
- OTHER KINDS OF ROCK MUSIC
- THE ROCK IN ITALY
- THE ROCK TODAY IN ITALY AND ABROAD
- TECHNICAL TERMS OF THE ROCK
- GLOSSARY OF ARTISTS AND MUSICAL GENES

PRESENTATION

Wave Of The Rock is a book of non-fiction, in which we will talk about how it can be seen from the same title, of music, mainly of rock music and the musical genres closest to it.

More precisely, we will deal with the following musical genres:

Foundations of Rock: Rock Blues, Rock and roll, Rock;

Evolutions: Hard Rock and Heavy Metal, Melodic Rock (or Soft Rock), Psychedelic Rock, Grunge and Punk Rock, Pop Rock and New Wave, Thrash Metal;

Further Evolutions and Transformations: Alternative Rock, Progressive Rock, Gothic Rock, and Electronic Rock.

Jumps or references to other genres are not excluded.

Everything will be treated with a deep and careful analysis from an instrumental point of view, gradually citing and speaking also of all the greatest protagonists who have marked these genres and indicating their most famous and most beautiful songs.

Written by **Salvatore Bellassai.**

In the next chapter, the second of **Wave Of The Rock** we will talk a little bit about the history of the birth of Rock.

HISTORY AND BIRTH OF THE ROCK

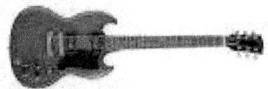

The term **Rock** in English means rock, but also to swing, swing, move, which is mainly indicating a type of music with a hard and strong sound capable of making people move and shake.

The origins of **Rock** and **Blues** music go back to the birth of very popular Afro-American songs, which had a particular tone and rhythm. These songs then evolved with the inclusion of musical instruments and led in the 50s to the birth of the two styles in the United States.

The birth of the **Blues** is mainly due to the rhythmic and improvisation skills of the Africans who joined the music of the whites when they came to the United States due to slavery. In Europe this type of mixture gave rise to **Jazz**. From a variation above all of the blues, **Rock and roll** was born mainly in the speed of the rhythm, from a harder, raw and energetic sound of Rock and roll with more aggressive lyrics **Rock** was born.

A fundamental characteristic of nascent Rock music concerned above all the lyrics, which dealt with social and protest themes against society.

A tendency to go against the tide very characteristic of the style, especially in **Grunge** and **Punk Rock**, which also gave birth to the birth of many cultural movements including Rockers, and the Punk culture, which is still widespread in young people today, which they immediately stand out in their way of dressing.

What distinguishes this genre from an instrumental point of view is a sound that sees the use mainly of the amplified electric guitar, accompanied by electric bass and drums that began to create that hard, strong and incisive sound of which it originated word. Several musical bands have also inserted the keyboard, but always in a minimal part in this type of songs.

The blues (*rock blues in this case*) and *rock and roll* played with the equipment referred to in the previous paragraph, can be defined in a pure state, to be well distinguished from those played for dancing, much more sophisticated and with the addition of many other instruments and sounds, which in common with the first ones have only the rhythm.

In the next chapter we will talk about the **first protagonists.**

THE FIRST PROTAGONISTS

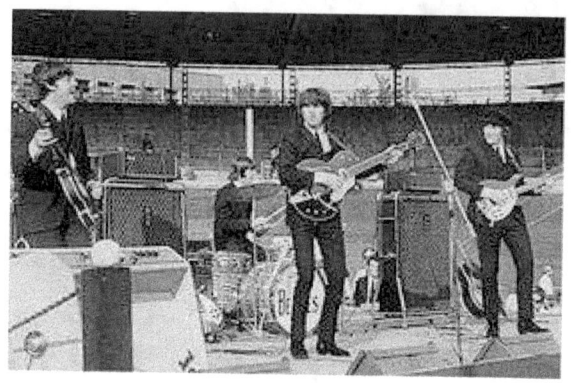

Here in the photo we see one of the Biggest and most discussed British bands of all time, we are talking about **the Beatles**, who in the sixties began to give life to a genre that was certainly fundamental in getting to rock today. We see two typical sixties guitars, bass and drums, guitars used mainly with clean sound, but which have created many beautiful songs, *Help!, A Hard Day's Night, Ticket to Ride, Paperback Writer*.

Subsequently over the years the band has evolved into other musical genres, introducing the piano and moving more towards Pop music, up to writing the songs that we all know, **Imagine**, **Let it Be**, **Yesterday** and others.

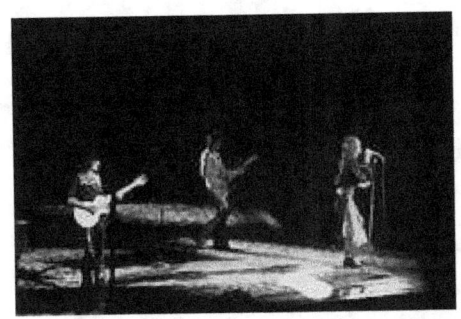

The **Rolling Stones**, another epochal English band, The instruments used are the same as the Beatles, electric guitars, electric bass, drums. Unlike their English cousins, however, in addition to playing Blues, Rock and roll, in their songs they made a lot of use of the distorted guitar, confirming a strong, incisive and scratchy sound, typical of Rock music. Among the most popular songs **Satisfaction,** *Start me up, she's a Reinbow.*

The two British bands after studying the US sounds, they composed their own songs that made them protagonists of the world scene.

Elvis Presley, **Jerry Lee Lewis** and **Chuck_Berry_** were also forerunners of the genre in the United States, also playing a lot of Blues and Rock and Roll.

Introduced the distorted sound of the guitars, they began to compose as well as scratchy chords also melodic solos that enchanted, here with others came **Jimi Hendrix** and **Santana** who between the late 60s and early 70s consecrate rock music.

Santana immediately highlights one of the characteristics of rock, the mix, that is the ability to easily combine with other musical genres. Mixing it with Latin music he played *Latin Rock.*

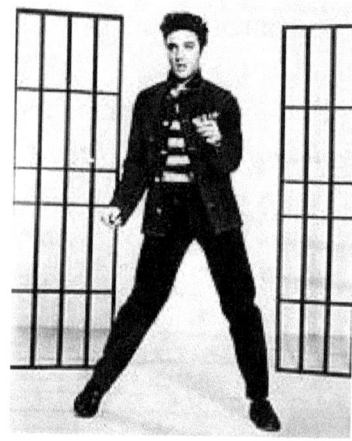
Elvis Presley

From the basic sounds of the style many other genres and sub-genres gradually developed: *Hard Rock* and *Heavy Metal*, *Melodic Rock* (or *Soft Rock*), *Psychedelic Rock*, *Grunge* and *Punk Rock*, *Pop Rock* and *New Wave*, *Thrash Metal* and others, who had their great **protagonists**.

PROTAGONISTS (Rock Blues and Rock and Roll)

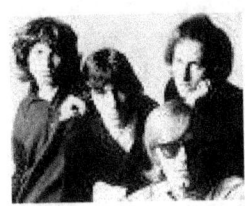
Doors, USA

Let's start with Rock Blues; After the precursors Rolling Stone, **Led Zeppelin**, in part the Beatles, many have thrown themselves into this genre, but among the biggest and most charismatic we certainly include **the Doors**, the Blues rhythms are evident in the most famous songs, *Love Street*, *People are Strange* and especially *Roadhouse blues*. The sound was formed not only by the voice of the leader Jim Morrison, by electric guitar, drums and by a great keyboard player, who besides an impressive agility in the execution of very fast notes (remember the intro of *Light my Fire*), with the hand left also played the bass part of the songs. For their way of playing certain songs, with long, almost endless solos of both guitar and organ and rhythm changes, they have also gained a place in the **Psychedelic Rock** genre, which we will discuss later.

Eric Clapton also played rock music but *Chuck Berry* called him the lord of the Blues, in fact, his influence on this musical style was great, and the song *Layla* is an example of his ability to express it.

Rock Blues also played **Led Zeppelin**, despite their most famous song *Stairway to Heaven*, made with wonderful arpeggios of amplified acoustic guitars, it did not have these characteristics.

In 1978 the comedians *John Belushi* and *Dan Aykroyd* founded the **Blues Brothers,** here in addition to interpret the film "*The Blues Brothers*" they will write many songs with rhythm in Blues, including in 1980 a reinterpretation of *Sweet Home Chicago* by **Robert Johnson**, one of the founders of Blues music.

In Rock and Roll (considered one of the fathers) **Jerry Lee Lewis** introduced the piano, playing it with the skill and agility necessary to perform this musical style.

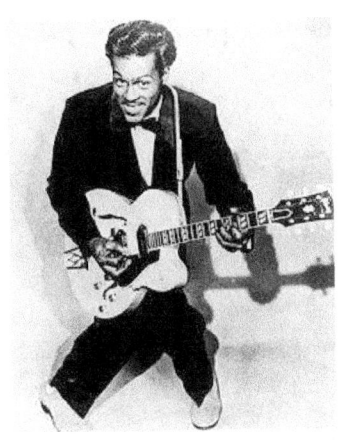

Chuck Berry

In the photo **Chuck Berry** was the one who wrote one of the most famous and played Rock and Roll style songs in the world, *Johnny B. Goode.*

Very played song also by the first Bands that overlook the scene of Rock music, a very useful song for acquiring agility in the use of instruments.

Guns N 'Roses played this style very heavily, making extensive use of distorted guitars, Alice Cooper's *Caught in a Dream* and a beautiful *Rock and Roll* style song.

Surely in these articles I will forget many interpreters, but I have chosen those that in my opinion have characterized the musical styles the most.

In the next chapter we will begin to talk **about the evolution of Rock** that gave birth to other musical genres.

EVOLUTIONS OF THE ROCK

Both in England and in the US it began to appear in the early 70s, but it marked all the 80s and 90s, let's talk about **Hard Rock**. From the genres described in the previous articles, we start to use guitars with distorted sound more and more, among the first we have seen the *Rolling Stones*. But not only for the solos but also for the rhythm, the bass played with less notes, riffs and scales, performed only in particular points of the song, is used to mark the rhythm of the song often with particular effects, many times with an almost metallic sound.

From *Hard Rock* then **Heavy Metal** was born, with a louder volume, rhythm and intensity of sound, complete absence of Piano, and the guitars that were usually two, were often both used with distortion. The boundary between *Hard rock* and *Heavy Metal* was always thin, so much so that often the two were identified in one thing, but in Hard Rock you can still distinguish the origins of Rock and Roll, while the way to perform the song Heavy Metal acquires a new identity of its own.

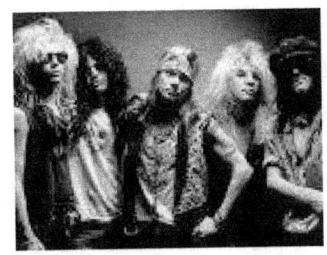 **Guns N'Roses**

Here is a photo of the American band of **Guns N 'Roses,**

two protagonists and drivers of this band were the singer **Axl Rose**, and **Slash** the guitarist, protagonists in the 80s and 90s of the world Hard rock scene. They tried to play Metal music, many call it a Heavy Metal band, but in most of their songs and the way to perform them is *Rock and roll.*

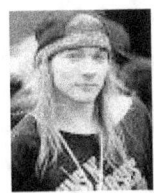 **Axl Rose**

The voice with Axl's Scratching falsetto at the high points of the songs is indistinguishable.

They were also able to play Soft rock, medium-slow and very melodic songs, where in most of the song the distortion is abandoned (except in the refrains), for poignant arpeggios, adding very special effects on the guitar; Truly complicated arpeggios that in certain points of the song developed not only on the chord but also according to riffs and particular scales.

Among these types of songs we remember ***Don't Cry, Civil War, November Rain***, in this last song as in many others of the band there is also the piano. Among the Hard Rock songs instead ***Welcome to the Jungle, You Could Be Mine, Paradise City***. A compromise between Hard Rock and Melodic Rock is ***Sweet Child O 'Mine.***

Other Hard Rock bands >>

OTHER HARD ROCK BANDS

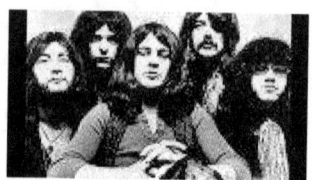

Deep Purple are an English band born in the early 70s, also members of *Hard Rock* and *Heavy Metal*. They distinguished themselves from other groups that played these genres because they inserted the use of keyboards, keyboards used with a particular organ effect; Just the way to use this instrument also gave a psychedelic connotation to the band, so much so that it was attributed to the Psychedelic Rock style.
Their performances often did not hesitate to mix the Blues. Among the most famous tracks ***Smoke on The Water***, known all over the world.

The type of distortion used on the guitar and its settings was fundamental in **Kiss**'s playing style.

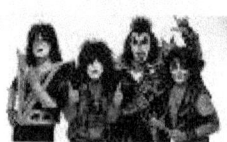
Kiss

Entering the *Hard Rock* scene in the early 70s in the USA, they too gave the way to be distinguished, their songs had a particular Rhythm, where the electric bass that distinguished them emerged, *I Was Made For Lovin 'You*, the most known, but in the 1979 Dynasty album, in addition to the one already mentioned, we also find other beautiful songs, *Sure Know Something*, *Magic Touch*, *Charisma* and many others.

The Australians **AC DC**, were characterized by the voice of their singers first Bon Scott, then Brian Johnson, very loud and scratchy voices, so much so that for the young Bands it was possible to imitate the sounds of the instruments, but it was very difficult to imitate the voices . They too were a band in love with *Rock and Roll* featured in many of their songs.

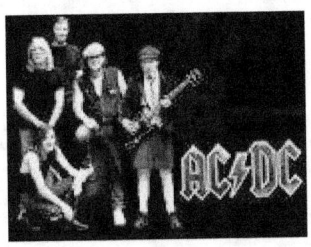

Among their most famous songs, first of all ***Back in Black***, this too one of the best known in the world, then **Hells Bells** who in their concerts introduced with the sound of bells, and the unmistakable ***Thunderstruck***, performed largely with a tapping technique only with the left hand.

In the next chapter of Wave Of The Rock we will talk about **Psychedelic Rock**.

PSYCHEDELIC ROCK AND PROGRESSIVE ROCK

For Psychedelic in general, we call that particular effect is defined as having particular drugs such as cannabis, but above all LSD on the organism, capable of altering the states of consciousness.

This term was used for music to indicate that those who played this genre, did it as if they were under the influence of these substances, which were able to inspire musicians and bring out unique sounds capable of evoking surreal atmospheres. Similarly the same effect was perceived by the listener, who entered an altered state as if he were under the influence of certain substances.

Now if all of this was only an identification or there was something else I will not go into the merits, the fact is that these bands have created truly exceptional songs, capable of evoking particular atmospheres, even for those who listened without taking drugs.

Both the **Doors** and the **Deep Purple**, of which we have already spoken in previous articles, entered the category of this type of genre. **Jimi Hendrix** was also part of it, but the ones that brought him to absolute perfection were in Great Britain in the late 60's the **Pink Floyd**.

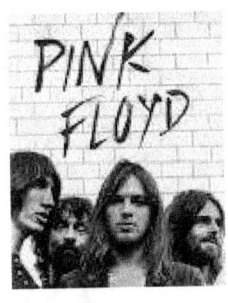

They managed to obtain this type of sound by introducing effects, in particular the deley on the guitar, and others on the keyboards such as the Echo, mixed with others, such as Reverberate, Sustain, Chorus etc .. One of their songs capable of evoking atmospheres particular is *Shine On You Crazy Diamond*, a song that goes beyond 10 minutes and where the predominant instrument is the keyboard. It starts, it is the background to the whole song first with one effect then with another. *Another Brick In The Wall*, and their symbolic song; *Wish You Were Here*, a little out of the canons of their kind, played with amplified electric and acoustic guitars, in *Run Like Hell* they made extensive use of the deley.

The song *Shine On You Crazy Diamond* rather than Psychedelic Rock, was a subgenre of this style, in fact it was much more complex instrumentally, with extensive use of keyboards, and then the long duration of the song gave it a **Rock Progressive** connotation, in fact *Pink Floyd* they also played this genre.

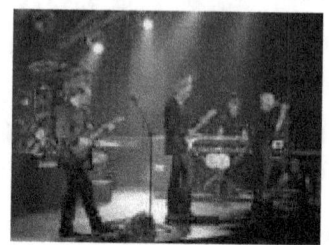 **Genesis**

Rock Progressive also played in Great Britain and at about the same time **Genesis**. In their songs through keyboard effects or with actual instruments, they introduced orchestral instruments (String, transverse flutes etc ...), and the duration of their best known songs was very long; These were all **Progressive features**. The song *The Musical Box* in the longest version was over 20 minutes long. Other known songs: *Carper Crawler*, *Genesis*, and *Mama*, the latter of shorter duration.

The next chapter will deal with **Grunge** and **Punk Rock**.

GRUNGE AND PUNK ROCK

I wanted to put these two genres together because they are very similar. First of all for the essentiality of the instruments used, often only drums, bass and guitar, and complete renunciation of the effects on the latter.

Not only did this have in common, the lyrics of the songs, characterized by a form of denunciation and protest against the society, culture and politics of the moment. This form of protest was unleashed above all in the refrains, which were angry and screamed, without losing the intonation of the song.

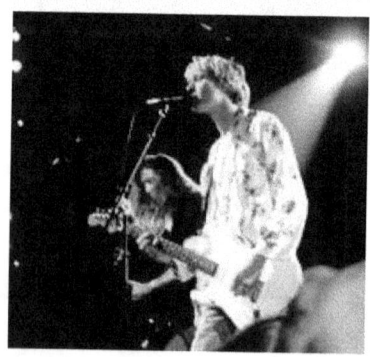 **Nirvana, USA.**

Total expression of *Grunge* music was the

Nirvana, Americans, appeared in the late 1980s and remained on the scene until the mid 1990s.

Who is not a musician and listens to them feels a completeness of the song, thinking who knows how many members were behind it. But as in one of their longest concerts, there were only three elements. Thanks to the singer and leader **Kurt Cobain** (highlighted in the photo), who in addition to singing with crazy energy, also played the guitar.

While singing, he played this instrument performing very complex songs, some with an infinite number of chords, such as *Lithium*. He also took care of all the solos, arpeggios, riffs, and anything else needed to perform the song.

Their songs, they were many and always captivating in their way of performing them, never tired, so much so that often their concerts were very long and endless. They continued to play beyond the limits becoming more and more angry, sometimes they went as far as hysteria, ending up breaking their musical instruments, or ending the concert almost passed out from fatigue. They too were a legend of Rock, in addition to the previously mentioned song, we remember other famous songs, first of all *Smells Like Teen Spirit*, then *Come As You Are*, *Silver*, *Polly*, but there are many more.

Punk Rock like *Grunge* used essential instruments, the text contents were violent and often of political protest, the songs did not last long. The most famous of this genre were **Sex Pistol** and **The Clash** in Britain, **Patti Smith** and **Green Day** in the United States, although the latter had a tendency to mix *Pop music*.

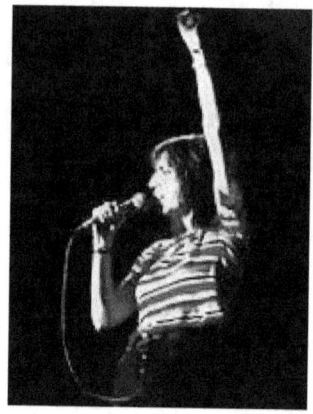
Patti Smith

As in *Patti Smith*'s songs, the Punk Rock lyrics were charismatic and very strong, sending the message to the people with power, but the musicality assumed an aggressive connotation later.

Characteristic of these songs was the increase in intensity, sound volume and voice as the song progressed, an example is the song **Gloria** of **Patti Smith**. It was the vocal determination in expressing the texts that characterized the **Punk style**.

The suggestive song by **Clash**, *London Calling*, did not have excessively loud sounds.

In the next chapter **Heavy Metal** and **Thrash Metal**.

HEAVY METAL AND THRASH METAL

We saw in the previous chapter that Rock reached its maximum expression in musical texts with *Punk Rock* and *Grunge*.

With **Thrash Metal** (*Heavy Metal* Subgenre) it reached the maximum power for what concerns the sonorities, making it complex and also with the appearance of Horror, also for the way to use the voice. **Metallica** (Los Angeles 1981) managed to create this style by applying a type of distortion to the atypical sounding guitar, different from that of the other styles. This type of effect made the Palm mute technique on the guitar very powerful, which in some stages of the song was as if beating and sharp sounds were heard (hence the term Thrash). The tracks with very fast stages had short sudden changes of rhythm and drum counter-times, especially during some types of solos.

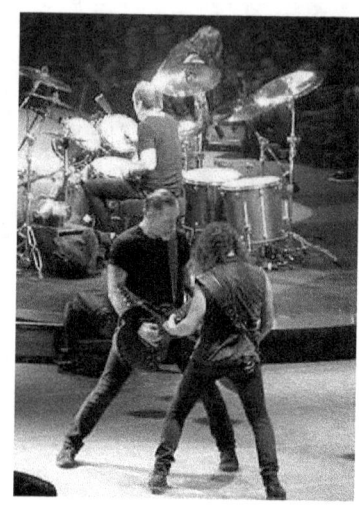

Metallica

As we see in the photo there was a great understanding between the singer and the guitarist, so much so that they performed some solos together and performed the same and identical notes, creating a captivating and particular sound typical of their genre.

They did not abandon *Heavy Metal*, in fact, they wrote many songs of this genre, and also of Soft Rock, **Nothing Else Matters** was an example. Other tracks **Enter Sandman, Fade to Black.**

The themes of the **Thrash** texts were more or less those of Rock, of protest. But here more against humanity's misdeeds during history towards men and towards the environment (*Metallica*).

Others spoke of the same Metal and the exaltation it caused in those who played it in those who listened to it, the same *Metallica*, and **Anthrax**. Others dealt with Horror and occult **Megadeth** themes.

Thrash Metal was very important role for the birth of even more extreme Metal genres such as *Death Metal* and *Black Metal*.

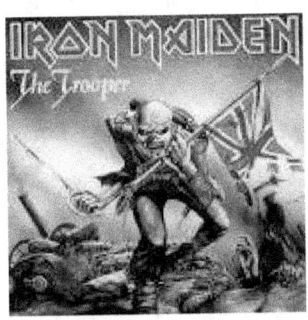

Iron Maiden (Great Britain 1975) called Heavy Metal Group, in fact they were. The untying of their way is evident playing from Hard Rock and its origin. Rhythm changes were their characteristic, choruses with distorted chords performed without rhythm, and they performed very difficult and fast solos, with an infinite number of notes. They also performed solos on two guitars like *Metallica*.

They wrote many *Thrash Metal* songs or a variant of this genre, however Thrash if they were not really for the sounds they were certainly for what they wanted to express, especially in their covers (see photos on the previous page). Songs to mention: **Fear of The Dark, Two Minutes to Midnight**, they also played Soft Rock with **Wasting Love**.

Another fundamental characteristic of *Heavy Metal* that differs it from *Hard Rock* is the way in which the singer expresses the themes of the lyrics, often with a very loud and more aggressive voice. In addition to the Iron Maiden, this we can see it in the **Black Sabbath**, and in some songs of the **Aerosmith**, *Hard Rock* band, which in **Shela** remember *Heavy Metal*.

The next topic in this book will be **Pop Rock** and **New Wave**.

POP ROCK AND NEW WAVE

The **New Wave** style developed from evident influences of the *Punk Rock* style that we have already talked about in previous chapters. This musical style however differed from Punk music because it was very close to Pop music. Precisely for this reason, consequently, it was also very close to **Pop Rock**.

In general with these two terms we indicate a popular music genre that is that unlike Rock, it embraces a wider audience, almost like pop music. The themes of the texts are often not excessively complex, which also concerned everyday life, with passages that can sometimes be danced.

The sounds of the instruments were very close to those of Rock music, but here the keyboards and synthesizers were inserted, which managed to give the songs a special touch, capable of also creating particular atmospheres (**Cold Play**), but which did not take Psychedelic characteristics. In some songs the rhythms were those of Pop music (**Depeche Mode**).

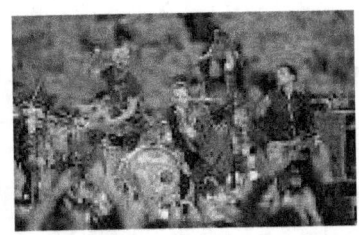 **Cold Play**

Cold Play are the most recent English group, (London 1997). For the type of sound they kept very close to Rock music, they didn't use the synthesizer very much, but they used keyboards. Singer **Chris Martin** played both the guitar but also the piano. Among the most beautiful songs *Hardest part*, *Yellow*, *Scientist*, *Paradise*, *Low*.

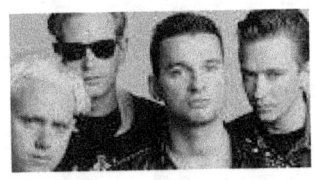 **Depeche Mode**

Although they never turned their attention away from the *Blues* and *Rock*, I **Depeche Mode** (UK 1980) with the voice of **Dave Gahan**, for the rhythm of many of their songs and use of synthesizers they were closer to **Pop music**.

Policy of Truth, was such a song, as *Never Let Me Down Again*. A song that took connotations very close to Rock was Useless. The symbol song *Enjoy The Silence*.

After a long essence from the main scenes, they showed their attachment to Rock in 2004 with a remake of *Enjoy The Silence* giving the song more rock and less pop semblance of the first version, then in 2006 other hits with *Dream On* and *Precious*.

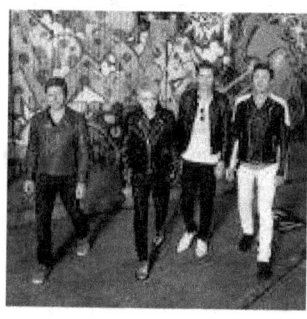

Duran Duran

English band, they also made use of synthesizers, and for the rhythms of many songs just like Depeche Mode, **Duran Duran** got very close to Pop music. They also approached Dance music more precisely **Dance Rock**, just because many songs were danceable. They were also good musicians for this in their live concerts, especially the *Duran Duran* of the last 2004 appearances, not using synthesizers, but only of keyboards, guitars, bass and drums, they approached Rock music a lot.

Among the songs of this type ***What's happen tomorrow*** from 2004. Other songs ***Ordinary World, Serious, The Reflex***.

Sting's Police are also the protagonists of the Pop Rock scene. One of the most beautiful songs they wrote ***Every Breath You Take*** (1983) contributed to their great success.

In America, the **Beach Boys** started with *Rock & roll*, but then they expressed a *Pop Rock* focused on vocal harmonies and having summer, surfing, Californian girls, and car racing as their themes.

Groups with other Rock features >>

BANDS WITH OTHER ROCK FEATURES

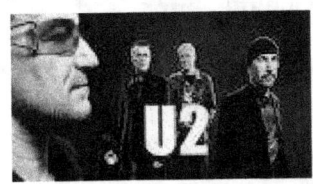

U2 are an Irish band, as well as with the magnificent voice of their Leader Paul David Hewson in art **Bono**, they got their indistinguishable style with the skill of their Guitarist.

This is also thanks to the abundant effects that he put on the guitar, reverbs, chorus and deley above all. In many of their songs they also helped with the synthesizer.

It were also called a *Post-Punk* or *New-Wave* band, eventually labeled it as a band playing **Alternative Rock**.

Songs: *In the Name of Love*, the best known together with *One*, *Lemon* (song taken from the Zooropa album, where the help of the synthesizers is heard), *Beautiful Day* and *Vertigo*. We can define the latter as a classic Rock song.

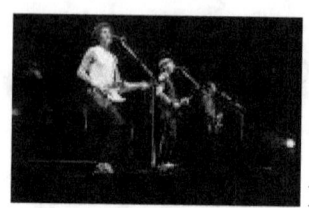
Dire Straits, English band

Dire Straits also made *Rock Blues* and other styles, but the way of playing of the singer and guitarist **Mark Knopfer** gave their most famous songs an unmistakable style.

In fact he played the guitar with an almost clean sound, and he did not use the pick, not only for the chords, but also for all the passages on the instrument.

This technique allowed him to play several notes at the same time using the fingers of his hand and perform very particular slides. Even for the solos of the songs, he did without the pick. *Sultans Of Swing* (The Very Best Of) the symbolic song of this band that had these characteristics.

It is not very easy to classify their musical style, they had many influences from pop music, but in the end in the type of rhythms of the guitar, clean without distorted sound, a country style emerged that played a lot in the clubs together with the *blues* and *Rock and Roll*.

Dire Straits' style was not defined as *alternative Rock* as that of *U2*, but I wanted to put in this article those groups that distinguished themselves for their way of playing rock, and obtained a great success.

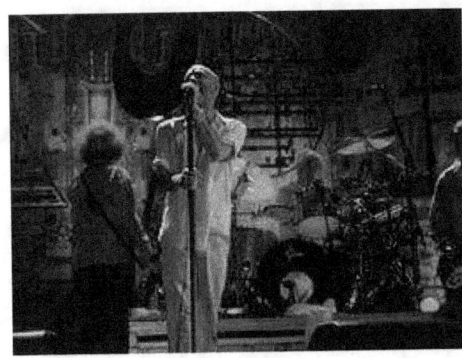

R.E.M.

U2 for the abundant effects, Dire Straits for the technique used, but there was another band that came out of the canons of traditional Rock and that created a very special sound while remaining within the Rock music.

The **R.E.M.** they were a symbol of **alternative Rock**, because they had the courage to not conform to the sound of the period, and to create a sound characterized by electro-acoustic Folk guitars, both for the rhythms, but also for the solos and for the riffs; They also used keyboards for light String backgrounds.

producing themselves, they began to make themselves heard on university radio at American colleges but gradually they came out to sell millions of records all over the world. Popular songs: ***Losing My Religion, Drive, Imitation Of Live, Leaving New York***.

In the next chapter we keep talking about **Alternative Rock**.

ALTERNATIVE ROCK

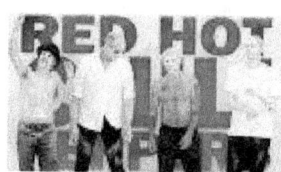 I Red Hot Chili Peppers from Los Angeles

Red Hot Chili Peppers like Nirvana, their sound was complex but formed only by three instruments, electric guitar, bass and drums. They also didn't over load the effects guitar. To bring out excellent musical pieces with this way of playing, you really must have a lot of imagination and be great artists.

They differed from *Nirvana* precisely in the way of expressing the messages in the texts, and in the rhythm of the passages close to the Funk. In fact, while Nirvana screamed in the refrains, the outburst of the Red Hot Chili Peppers often resulted in ripping their lyrics, their style was also called *Funk rock* and *Rap Rock*.

Hits: *Californication*, *Charlie*, *Dani California*, *By The Way*, *Hump De Bumb*, *Tell me Baby*, Snow.

Another difference with *Nirvana* was that the singer did not play any instrument, therefore free to move, jump, dance on stage.

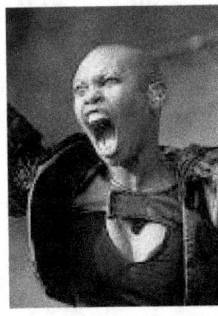
Skin

Skunk Anansie (Great Britain) also this band created its own sound with only three instruments, the use of the synthesizer was minimal. The singer **Skin** (which we see highlighted in the photo) was also free of tools and could move on stage involving people with her Charisma. The sounds were powerful enough, but also the lyrics, with angry political protests.

Their genre was not defined only as *Hard Rock*, especially for the hybrid and unpredictable rhythms, with funk, blues, reggae and Hip hop influences. They also joined the **Alternative Rock.**

Hits: ***Hedonism, Lately, Weak.***

came from Seattle Pearl Jam like Nirvana were influenced by that environment and therefore by the *Grunge* and *Punk* currents, in their style we find a bit of everything: *Punk, Grunge, Heavy Metal, Hard Rock*. Their singer had a very particular voice;

The Grunge style from which they left was different from that of their fellow citizens because it was influenced by the other styles described above.

Then to this by adding their nonconformist and anticommercial attitude, we can also define them an ***Alternative Rock*** band. Among their somg ***Jeremy*** 1991.

In the next chapter: **Dark Rock** and **Gothic Rock** >>

DARK ROCK AND GOTHIC ROCK

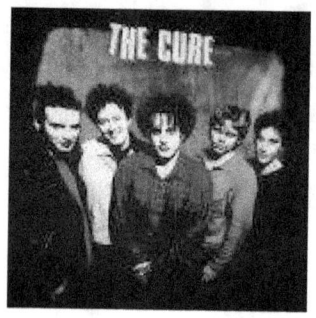

The Cure English band also had excellent musicians. The singer played the guitar, the first guitarist used a lot of effects and Deley. In their live concerts and songs, with the use of keyboards and the effects on guitars, they managed to evoke fascinating and particular atmospheres of the world of night and nightlife. Another characteristic of their sound was the bass used with the pick that took a characteristic sound. The gloomy and introspective texts perfectly suited the sounds, this style of them was called **Gothic Rock**, or **Dark Rock**.

They later abandoned the use of keyboards. Despite this they composed other beautiful songs, and did not lose that particular feature described before. This thanks the effects of the first guitar and the way it coordinated with the bass, which with the singer's particular voice always created unique sounds.

With the return of the keyboardist, they continued to do live concerts, of which they are masters, fully recreating all their songs on stage, despite their complexity.

Songs to suggest: **Lullaby, Love Song, Wrong Number, Close To Me, A Forest, Inbetween Days, Burn, Fashion Street.**

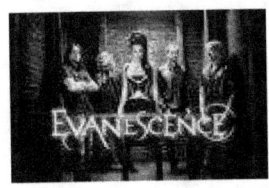

Evanescence (Little Rock, United States) also became popular for this type of music, still on stage until 2011. In their sonorities they made much use of distortion on the guitar, there was no lack of keyboards and their effects, and the piano. They often used the piano, which usually appeared when the volume of the song was decreasing, and then disappeared when the song increased in intensity again. The mix of all these instruments plus the singer's voice created the **Gothic-Dark** sounds.

The themes of the texts were perfectly suited to the sound, in fact, they often spoke of secrets, various mysteries and of religion, without however (as they specified) wanting to preach, but express only what they felt.

Songs: **Bring me to life, My Immortal, What You Want, Lost In Paradise, The Other Side, Sick.**

What differentiated *Dark Rock* from *Gothic Rock* was the way of singing, Gothic was characterized more by a female voice, slow and dreamy, and here Evanescence expressed it in some songs, such as Secret Door.

In the next chapter: **Electronic Rock.**

ELECTRONIC ROCK

This genre of music combines Rock with electronic music, and can have many facets, variations and styles. This depends on what type of Rock joins electronics. Some of these variants are the *Synth Pop* which comes from a fusion with *Pop Rock*, the most catchy. *SynthPunk*, or much more complex, experimental, and less commercial **Industrial Rock**.

In previous articles we have seen that many bands made use of synthesizers. There are those who used it very little and only for some songs, such as *Skunk Anansie, Duran Duran, U2*. Others made a much wider use of it such as **Depeche Mode**, for this reason, in addition the *Pop Rock* genre, it was also attributed to them **Electronic Rock**.

To perfectly play this style beyond the Voice, Guitars, bass, drums and keyboards, synthesizers, a Sampler to sample many types of sounds, noises and instruments even better, and the electronic drums.

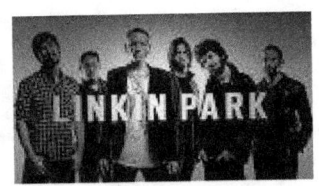

After the first already mentioned, other bandss famous for this type of Rock we remember first of all the Americans **Linkin Park** and their well-known song *In The End* (2003), but also many others that sold millions and millions of Discs all over the world.

Other foreign bands *Pendulum, Nine inch Nails, Kasabian.*

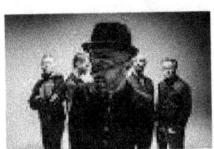 **Subsonica**

In Italy formed in 1996, we have the **Subsonica** group from Turin who played this genre; Among the most beautiful songs, ***Tutti i miei sbagli, Nuova ossessione, Incantevole.***

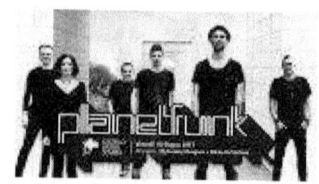

In 1999 **Planet Funk** entered the scene, many beautiful songs *Inside All The People*, *Every Day*, *Who Said*, in the style of Electronic Rock in 2009 the song *Lemonade*.

Bee Gees between Pop, Disco Music and Rock >>

BEE GEES, BETWEEN POP, DISCO MUSIC E ROCK

We had said in the presentation that jumps or references to other musical styles were not excluded. We take advantage of this in this chapter talking about another group that has made music history all over the world, we are talking about the **Bee Gees**. The three brothers of British origin moved to Australia and it was there that they began their musical career.

The **Gibb** brothers from an early age stood out for their vocal talent, later collaborating with each other began to write several songs.

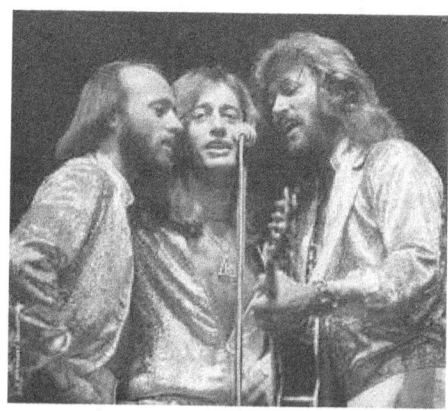
Bee Gees

Able to play instruments such as keyboards and guitars, two other members joined them, a guitarist and a drummer.

After completing the training, the group was also ready for live performances. The characteristic of the most famous songs was the falsetto voice of the three brothers, who by combining the various tones merged into a perfect mix, creating a unique vocal style.

Most of the lyrics were carefree, enhancing the fun, the holidays, the dance, the women and the love. Precisely for this reason, together with their sounds, they were considered one of the largest and most influential groups of *Pop music* and the first *Disco Music* of the 70s.

In 1967 inspired by the **Beach Boys**, for their essentiality of the instruments in some songs, where guitars and keyboards emerged, they also played different variations of rock music, in particular they approached folk Rock. They also attempted *Progressive Rock* that we have already talked about, and *Techno-Rock*.

In the mid-70s they turned decidedly towards *Disco Music*, the style with which they made their greatest hits; Here they brought with them the unmistakable sounds of the rhythm of the guitar, and the special organ and string backgrounds of the keyboards.

Among the most beautiful songs: ***Stayin 'Alive***, ***Night Fever***, ***Jive Talkin'***, ***You Should Be Dancing***, ***More Than a Woman***, and the poignant love song ***How Deep Is Your Love***.

Next chapter: **Glam Rock** >>

GLAM ROCK

The term **Glam Rock** does not refer exactly to the type of sound, but above all to clothing, to the way of posing on stage, and also to the themes of the lyrics. More exactly, it takes its name from "Glamor" a way of dressing with a very nice, colorful and showy look, often sexually ambiguous, just like the attitude on stage or in the videos of the protagonists of this genre.

Two great exponents of this musical genre were in England **The Queen** and **David Bowie**. *The Queen* did not have a precise musical genre, because they were influenced by many styles. Called a Rock band, they mainly played Rock, not very heavy *Hard Rock*, *Pop Rock*, **Dance Rock**, and when they introduced the synthesizer also *SinthPop*. Experiencing the above incision of their voices (making them appear like a large choir), they also approached the *Gospel*. Thanks to the skill of the Band and its famous guitarist *Brian May*, (but also of *Freddie* who was an excellent pianist) they were able to play live concerts. They were found to be bizarre especially by the front man **Freddie Mercury**, in the way of dressing and posing on stage and in videos, playing on sexual ambiguity, *the Queen* were called as a **Glam Rock** band.

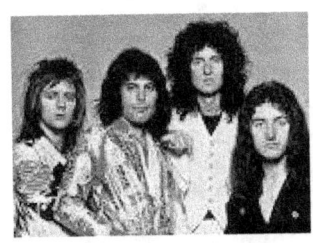 **The Queen**

I Want to Break Free is one of the songs where all the members of the Band dressed as women playing the role of housewives in a fun video.

The hits all know them, because like the *Beatles* and the *Rolling Stones* they sold millions and millions of albums. ***We Are the Champions, Somebody to Love, We Will Rock You, The Show Must Go On, A Kind of Magic, Radio Ga Ga*** (where they used the synthesizer), ***Don't 'Stop Me Now, Flash.***

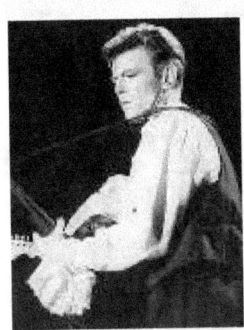 **David Bowie**

Another exponent of *Glam Rock* was **David Bowie**, like

Mercury performances on stage were bizarre, sometimes even shocking, ambiguous and impressive.

This genre was mainly theatrical, also in the way of showing the guitar, and the sound was not overly complex, but a simple Rock mixed with *Pop* influences and *Rock and Roll*. Despite this, the songs were no less than that of other styles and were also captivating.

Glam Rock joined *Mercury* and *Bowie* in a partnership that gave birth to a great single **Under Pressure** in 1981. **Starman, Let's Dance, Heroes** other great hits from Bowie.

Kiss, **The Cure** and **Alice Cooper** also interpreted this style.

Other genres of Rock music >>

OTHERS GENRES OF ROCK MUSIC

All genres of rock that we talked about in previous articles have always represented great artists. Having to make a choice of the various performers, we usually mentioned two or three.

There have been other genres of Rock that have also been played by the greats of the world scenes, but only partially during their career, or only in some songs, and therefore it was not possible to attribute their musical style.

Some well-known artists have been attributed these genres, however secondarily to others. For **Dire Straits**, **Bruce Springsteen** and **Bob Dylan** respectively, **Root rock**, **Heartland rock** and **Folk rock** were the main style for them.

Rockabilly: Born in the 50s, it is one of the first forms of Rock and Roll music, as well as *Blues* and *Rock and Roll* in the style, the **Country** is very present. Often this style was played with semi-acoustic guitars, instead of the electric bass the double bass was used. The rockabillies supporters had their own look, even in the hair cut, we remember the very popular ones of *Jerry Lee Lewis* and *Elvis Presley*.

Heartland rock: Very inspired by American folk music and with his strong communicative immediacy, **Bruce Springsteen** (nicknamed "The Boss"), was one of the greatest exponents of this style, characterized by the use of Folk guitars.

Folk Rock: This style is characterized by the fusion of rock with folk music in a broad sense, not only American, but also European. **Bob Dylan** was a representative, enriching him with his way of communicating and reaching people, that is, through words. In fact, he was also called a poet.

Root Rock: It was born in the 80s, from musical groups that gradually moved away from *pop music* for a return to the sounds of *classic rock*. Also here as the Rockabilly, in addition to the *Blues* and *Rock and Roll*, the Country style of the 50s and 60s was very present, and the sound of the semi-acoustic or electric guitars often used with clean sound.

Indie Rock: everyone reading the term can immediately think of a mix of rock music with Indian music, but in fact it is not so. *Indie Rock* is a genre that includes those bands that play *Alternative Rock*, wanting even more to detach themselves from the usual type of music, the one that record companies sometimes impose for their own profit.

Then from the term indie (an abbreviation of the English that stands for independence) bands not really well known preferredself-produce and promote yourself by leaving the money out of your own pocket in order to have the freedom to play the type of music you want without any limitation or restriction. This phenomenon began to spread even more after 2000. In Great Britain in the early nineties **Oasis** came on the scene, which was one of the symbol bands of the Indies (best known songs: ***Wonderwall, Wathever, Don't look back anger***).

Hardcore Punk: Subgenre of *Punk Rock*, it was born in the 80s. The characteristics of this genre were the high speed of the Rhythms, the shouting song, simple and distorted sounds. The texts were generally political and about the problems of contemporary society. This style was very important because it made a big contribution to the birth of *Trash Metal* and *Grunge*.

Acid Rock: It is nothing but a Psychedelic Rock played in a much more noisy and energetic way, **Jimi Hendrix** nor was he an interpreter. This genre was also very important, because like *Hardcore Punk*, it proved very important for the birth of other musical genres, in this case for *Heavy Metal*.

Noise Rock: Appeared in the 70s Noise Rock as from the same English word Noise (Noise) is a very noisy type of Rock, with distortions, repetitiveness of guitar riffs, where the instruments were more beaten than played.

This style wanted to upset the usual structure of the verse-refrain-solo songs, precisely with very repetitive stages of guitar performances. Voices were often used atonal.

Funk Rock, Rap Rock, Dance Rock: These three styles were born in the late 70s and early 80s from a fusion of Rock sounds with *Funk*, *Rap* and *Disco music*.

Sinth Pop: This musical style was obtained from those Pop or Pop Rock bands that began to make wider use of the Synthesizer;

Industrial Rock and Experimental Rock: Industrial Rock was born in the 70s, and comes from influences of the type of music produced by the *industrial records label*. In general, this term indicates a very particular type of music which is a mixture of the various Rock and Electronic Music genres. A very experimental mixture (Hence also the term *Experimental Rock*) of the sounds and of the typical Rock and l lyrics with 'Electronics. This style coincides more and more with *Experimental Rock* the more the results of the music produced are hybrid and unpredictable, with new and unique results.

Rock in Italy >>

ROCK IN ITALY

Thanks to the Sanremo festival in particular, Italy has a tradition of *light music* with themes of texts that usually concerned everyday life and love. The songs were easy to listen, intended for simple entertainment.

The first signs of Rock music, especially in sound, came with Edoardo Bennato, the piece *"Ok Italia"* is an example. Who really began to devote themselves to rock music **were Vasco Rossi, Litfiba** and **Luciano Ligabue**, in the mid-1980s. Then **Negrita, Timoria, Verdena, Negramaro** and others also arrived. *Stadio* remained in the middle between light music and Rock.

Litfiba already started moving in the early 1980s, but louder sounds came later.

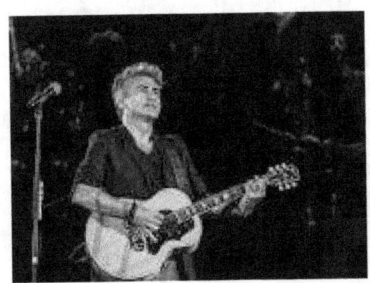

Luciano Ligabue

Personally I learned a lot in trying to play the songs of **Ligabue** and his *Band*, since they were very catchy, but at the same time also very complex (Let's talk about arpeggios, contrarpeggios, riffs etc ...).

On the characteristics of the sound there could be no doubt that that of Luciano and his Band was Rock, given the instruments. Guitars, not very full of effects but with the use of distortions, electric bass and drums, absence of the keyboard, which appeared slightly in some song.

He had two formations of musicians with whom he made great success, the first with the guitarist *Cottafavi*, with whom he played the first songs that made him known, then with *Fede Poggibollini* and *Mel Previte* who entered later. As for the lyrics, there were no strong protest tones, but often dealt with the exaltation of the Bands and the music. He was also attentive to delicate social issues such as those of the drug.

It is impossible to list the most beautiful songs because you would write a very long list, it is just a matter of choosing a few: ***Tra palco e realtà, Cosa vuoi che sia, Quella che non sei, Certe notti, Almeno Credo, Happy Hour, La linea Sottile, Il mio Pensiero.***

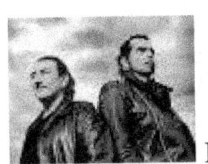
Pelù and Renzulli

Litfiba were the most powerful from the sound point of view, both in rhythmics, but also as regards the texts with many political messages, but they also spoke of the exaltation of the music and of the charge and energy it could give.

Here too, as Ligabue, it is only a matter of making a painful choice because mentioning all the successes would be an infinite list: ***El Diablo, Proibito, Lo Spettacolo, Terremoto, Fata Morgana, A denti stretti, Tutti fenomeni, Elettrica, Regina di Cuori***. The singer **Pierò Pelù** after the separation with the guitarist **Renzulli**, had many musicians in his band who took turns, The return of the two together gave inspiration for another great piece "***Sole nero***".

Vasco Rossi with slightly less evident rock sounds than Liga and *Pelù*, also dealt with delicate themes in his songs, in others if they did not have a protest tone, they were disappointed by the world and society. ***Liberi liberi, Siamo Soli, Io no, Come Stai, Il Mondo che vorrei, Vivere non è facile, Manifesto futurista, Eh già***, they are just some of his greatest successes.

Verdena distinguished themselves from the others because they managed to get out of a New Wave style and make *Grunge, Psychedelic* and *alternative Rock*. **Marlene Kuntz** also played *Alternative Rock*.

With a very powerful and complete Rock sound, Negrita made many beautiful songs (***Transalcolico, Provo a difendermi, Non ci guarderemo indietro mai, Bambole, In ogni atomo, Mama Maè, Hollywood***). The sound was characterized by the two guitars, often using effects such as wah-wah, and bottleneck to perform slides on the guitar, especially for solos. The texts dealt with stories and everyday problems of young people, love, alcohol, difficulties to overcome etc.

Senza vento, E' cosi facile, they are two beautiful songs written by **Timoria**.

Rock in Italy and abroad >>

ROCK TODAY IN ITALY AND ABROAD

Today there are many bands that play Rock music, while making excellent pieces, they are not managing to have the success of their predecessors. Also for this reason many people think that Rock has disappeared. Others argue that Rock has merged with *Pop*, so as to no longer distinguish the two genres.

In Italy the latest flurries of Rock come from *Piero Pelù* and his new formations. In the mid-2000s he wrote a very energetic album played on three instruments Guitar, Bass, Drums, and his Voice, Then the return with *Renzulli* and other songs. *Ligabue* also wrote other Rock pieces, the Arrivederci Mostro album in 2010 and other singles. The *Negrita* and *Negramaro* in many of their pieces abandoned the loud sounds. **Zu** are an Italian group in activity that play **Noise Rock**.

This summer we have seen that even *light music* has been put aside, for *Pop*, *Rap* and *Dance music*. We saw it in the songs of *Nek* and *J-AX*, *Mario Venuti* come, *Fabri Fibra* and *The journalists*.

Abroad, there are still many valuable bands around the scene, **Placebo, Smashings Pumpkis, Muse, Cold Play.**

What is going very fashionable is *Progressive Rock*, a subgenre of British *Psychedelic Rock* but much more complex in composition, the violin and the transverse flute often appeared. **Alternative Rock** is also still very popular, with **the** *Smashings Pumpkis* and ***Placebo***.

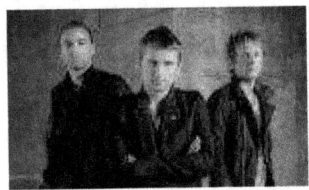
Muse, English Bands.

Speaking of *Alternative Rock* and *Progressive Rock*, an active group that represents them both are the Muses, known for the single *Times is Running Out*. The themes of their texts are quite complex Politics, Religion, Mysteries, War. In their Live performances they emotionally involve the public with very particular lighting scenes and with the energy and skill of the Band, from which emerges the *psychedelic style* that is incorporated into *Progressive Rock*. Last Album Drones (2015).

Alternative Rock and *Progressive Rock* have ended up also influence Metal, today many bands play *Alternative Metal* and *Progressive Metal*.

TECHNICAL TERMS OF THE ROCK

Here are the technical terms used in this blog in order to facilitate and make reading easier even for non-musicians:

Amplifier: Instrument that through speakers amplifies enhances the sound produced by a musical instrument.

Bottleneck: it is a 5-7 cm hollow cylinder to be inserted on the finger and which, sliding on the guitar strings, gives them a particular sound, used above all in genres such as country and blues.

Electric guitar: It is a type of guitar in which the vibration of the metal strings is detected by one or more pick-ups; the signal is then picked up at the output and conveyed to an amplifier so that the sound is audible.

Folk guitar: It is an acoustic guitar, that is, that the sound is reproduced by the vibrations of the soundboard. Unlike the classical guitar, it is designed to accommodate metal strings instead of nylon strings. All this causes a different sound, used in the execution of pieces of *modern music, blues, folk, rock* and, in general, of *light music*.

With the use of external pick-ups, or if already prepared, the sound can become even louder through the connection to amplifiers.

Chorus: Effect for guitars that gives the instrument more body in the sound. It is obtained by recording the sound of the guitar itself, and then mixing it with the original with a minimum delay, creating a sound similar to that of a chorus of multiple guitars.

Deley: Effect for guitar or other instruments that serves to record the sound and play it continuously with a certain delay, obtaining an echo of the sound until it fades. The delay can be regulated by special pedals.

Distortion: Electric guitar effect that changes the timbre, the dynamics is the duration of the sound, making it similar to that of an amplifier pushed beyond its possibilities, which saturates, distorts the sound, giving it the typical characteristics of rock music. This effect can be obtained with a special pedal, where you can adjust the volume, and more.

Echo: Ancient effect that Pink Floyd used to give more body and a characteristic sound to keyboards.

Flanger: Guitar effect that in addition to being able to create

Chorus and Deley, can reproduce various noises almost similar to the noise of a Jet taking off.

Palm Mute: Guitar technique which consists in damping the sound with the palm of the right hand, resting it lightly on the strings. The same hand that pinches the string, obtaining a characteristic and particular sound.

Riff: A particular musical passage is meant in the guitar, consisting of a succession of notes that frequently occurs within the song (often also at the beginning), characterizing it. The Riff is usually not very long and gives a strong expressiveness to the song. Sometimes it can be used as an accompaniment for most of its duration.

Reverb: It is similar to the deley, only while in the deley the echo effect is reproduced with a certain delay, we speak of more seconds, the *reverberation* reproduces the sound after a delay of fractions of a second making it very different from the first.

Pick-up: Electric device that allows you to transform the vibrations of the guitar strings into electrical impulses so that they can be transmitted to the amplifier to enhance its sound.

Sampler: instrument sampler that can be connected to a midi keyboard (or other electronic devices) so that you can play with many other types of musical instruments. There are also software now that does this on the computer.

Synthesizer: Very complex electronic instrument that is capable of generating, sampling and reproducing the sounds of any instrument, noises, and any other effects. It can be used during a concert by musicians to let that type of sound enter at the set time, automatically or under someone's command.

Slide: Guitar technique which consists of changing notes or chords by sliding your fingers on the keyboard.

String: Effect used mainly on keyboards to create a background for music, but also for other. Playing a musical chord, the String imitates a set of bow instruments, violins, violas, cellos etc ...

Tapping: is a guitar technique that allows you to play notes directly on the fretboard without plucking the strings, using the fingers of the right or left hand, or at the same time to be able to perform even more complex sounds and scales.

Wah-wah: Musical effect widely used on guitars giving it a sound similar to a whimper or meow.

GLOSSARY OF ARTISTS AND MUSICAL GENES:

AC DC: Hard Rock, Rock and roll (25,26);

Aerosmith: Hard Rock, Heavy Metal (40);

Alice Cooper: Rock, Rock and Roll, Blues (17,70);

Anthrax: Trash Metal (39);

Beach Boys: Rock & roll, Pop rock (45,65);

Beatles: Rock, Blues rock, Rock & roll, Pop (10,11,15,53);

Bee Gees: Disco Music '70, Pop, Rock, Rock elettr. (64,65,66);

Bennato Edoardo: Italian Rock (77);

Bob Dylan: Folk Rock, Rock & roll (72,73);

Black Sabbath: Heavy Metal (40);

Bruce Springsteen: Heartland Rock, Rockabilly (72,73);

Cold Play: Pop, Pop Rock, New Wave (42,43,82);

Chuck Berry: Rock and Roll (16,17);

David Bowie: Glam Rock (68,69,70);

Deep Purple: Hard Rock, Rock Psichedelico (24,28);

Depeche Mode: New Wave, Sinth Pop, Rock elettronico (42,43,44,60);

Dire Straits: Root Rock, Blues Rock, Country (48,49,72);

Doors: Blues, Rock Psichedelico (15,28);

Duran Duran: New Wave, Sinth Pop, Dance Rock (44,45,60);

Elvis Presley: Rock and Roll, Rockabilly, Blues (11,12,72);

Eric Clapton: Rock, Rock Blues (16);

Evanescence: Gothic Rock, Dark Rock (57,58);

Genesis: Rock Progressive, Pop Rock, Pop Progressive (30);

Green Day: Punk Rock, Pop Rock, Rock alternative (34);

Guns N' Roses: Hard Rock, Soft Rock, Rock&Roll (17,21,22);

Iron Maiden: Heavy Metal (39,40);

Jimi Hendrix: Rock, Psichedelic Rock, Acid Rock (12,28,74);

Jerry Lee Lewis: Rock and Roll, Rockabilly (11,16,72);

Kiss: Hard Rock; Glam Rock (24,25,70);

Led Zeppelin: Rock, Rock Blues; Melodic Rock (15,16);

Ligabue: Rock New Wave (77,78,79,82);

Linkin Park: Elettronic Rock (61);

Litfiba: Rock, New Wave (77,79,82);

Marlene Kuntz: Alternative Rock (80);

Megadeth: Trash Metal (39);

Metallica: Heavy Metal, Trash Metal (37,38,39);

Muse: Alternative Rock, Progressive Rock., Psichedelic Rock (82,83);

Negramaro: Rock, Pop Rock (77,82);

Negrita: Rock, Alternative Rock (77,80,82);

Nirvana: Grunge (32,33,52,53,54);

Oasis: Rock, IndieRock (74);

Patti Smith: Punk Rock (34,35);

Pearl Jam: Alternative Rock, Grunge, Hard Rock (54);

Pink Floyd: Psichedelic Rock, Progressive Rock (28,29,87);

Placebo: Alternative Rock, Gothic Rock (82,83);

Planet Funk: Elettronic Rock (62);

Police: Pop Rock (45);

Robert Johnson: Blues (16);

Red Hot Chili Peppers: Alternative Rock, Funk Rock, Rap Rock (52);

R.E.M.: Alternative Rock, Folk Rock (49,50);

Rolling Stones: Rock, Rock Blues (11,20);

Santana: Latin Rock, Blues Rock (12);

Sex Pistol: Punk Rock (34);

Skunk Anansie: Hard Rock, Altern Rock., Indie Rock (53,60);

Smashings Pumpkis: Alernative Rock (82,83);

Subsonica: Elettronicc Rock (61);

The Blues Brothers: Blues (16);

The Clash: Punk Rock (34,35);

The Cure: Dark Rock, Glam Rock (56,57,70);

The Queen: Glam Rock, Pop Rock, Sinth Pop, Dance Rock (68,69,70);

Timoria: Rock (77,80);

Vasco Rossi: Italian Rock (77,79);

Verdena: Psichedelic Rock, Grunge (77,80);

U2: Rock, Alternative Rock (47,49,60);

Zu: Noise Rock (82);

Conclusions and thanks

This book, read only once, is a fantastic adventure in rock music, from its birth to the present day; But if read several times, or studied, precisely because of the technical approach to this musical genre, it becomes a real manual. A very useful manual for those who are already experts to have even clearer ideas, but also very valuable for those who approach or already study a musical instrument. Especially in order to be able to choose and specialize in this path after the classic study of the instrument.

I was able to write this book thanks to the study of the guitar and piano, so thanks to the teachers. To the friends who made up the various bands I was part of, which allowed me to enrich the experience on my instruments, and at the same time let me know others, the bass, the drums etc ...

Thanks to all my fellow guitarists, singers and musicians who have not been part of my bands, from whom I have always learned new things.

Thanks to the web and Wikipedia inexhaustible sources of information that have allowed me to perfect the draft as much as possible, enriching it with many more details.

Finally thanks to the protagonists of this book, the Singers and the Bands, which I was able to study also thanks to the various concerts seen live and in the videos.

Written By **Salvatore Bellassai** in the year 2017-2018.

Printed in 2020 ;

***** *In the e-book format, use the document search box to find any topic, for example a singer, a band, a musical genre, a technical term etc ...*

****

COPYRIGHT **Salux SC&S** By *Salvatore Bellassai* (in art *Salvatore Lo Bello*);

Editor **Salux SC&S;**

It is absolutely forbidden to reproduce and distribute this book without authorization.

****